D0873928

THE GO-KART RACE

BY RACHEL BACH

AMICUS READERS AMICUS INK

amicus readers

Say Hello to Amicus Readers.

You'll find our helpful dog, Amicus, chasing a ball—to let you know the reading level of a book.

1

Learn to Read

High frequency words and close photo-text matches introduce familiar topics and provide ample support for brand new readers.

2

Read Independently

Some repetition is mixed with varied sentence structures and a select amount of new vocabulary words are introduced with text and photo support.

3

Read to Know More

Interesting facts and engaging art and photos give fluent readers fun books both for reading practice and to learn about new topics.

Amicus Readers and Amicus Ink are imprints of Amicus
P.O. Box 1329, Mankato, MN 56002
www.amicuspublishing.us

Editor: Wendy Dieker
Designer: Tracy Myers
Photo Researcher: Aubrey Harper

Library of Congress Cataloging-in-Publication Data
Names: Bach, Rachel, author.
Title: The go-kart race / by Rachel Bach.
Description: Mankato, Minnesota : Amicus, [2017] | Series: Let's Race
Identifiers: LCCN 2015043981 (print) | LCCN 2015046156 (ebook) | ISBN
 9781607539131 (Library Binding) | ISBN 9781681510378 (eBook) | ISBN
 9781681521329 (paperback)
Subjects: LCSH: Karting--Juvenile literature.
Classification: LCC GV1029.5 .B34 2017 (print) | LCC GV1029.5 (ebook)
 | DDC 796.7/6--dc23
LC record available at http://lccn.loc.gov/2015043981

Photo Credits: Travis VanDenBerg/Alamy Stock Photo cover; TachePhoto/Shutterstock 3, 12-13; Koji Aoki/Aflo/Corbis 4; Carl Lyttle/Getty 6-7; imageBROKER/Alamy 8-9; Avid Creative, Inc./iStock 11; Maurizio Borsari/Aflo/Corbis 15; Margo Harrison/Shutterstock 16

Printed in the United States of America.

HC 10 9 8 7 6 5 4 3 2 1
PB 10 9 8 7 6 5 4 3 2 1

The go-kart race is today.
The drivers get ready.

Carly puts on a helmet.

She puts on gloves.

The green
flag waves.
The race begins.
Off they go!

Bella goes around
the corner.
Dylan passes her
on lap two.

Abby tries to
catch up.
There are only
10 laps left.

John spins out.

Oh no!

It is a close finish.
Carly wins!

PARTS OF A GO-KART

engine

steering wheel

tires